AF335437

BALLADS
of a
BENCH WARMER

David Pierce

caislan press

Box 28371, San Jose, California 95159

BALLADS OF A BENCH
WARMER

Copyright 1982 by David Pierce

All rights reserved.

Printed in the United States of America.

Library of Congress Catalogue Card Number: 82-71855

ISBN: 0-937444-04-9

CAISLAN PRESS

CONTENTS

To The Old Gang

And the good times
Abrazos,
Dave

P.S.
And the good girls
like Carol.
x x

IN CHINA SEAS

The old man sits in the Chinese takeaway,
Watching 'Policewoman' and boiling peas.
The picture on the wall has some Chinese writing,
He says that it means, 'In China Seas . . .'

In China seas . . .
The waters that sailors dread . . .
In China seas . . .
In Shanghai they paint the junks red . . .
Red for protection? I do not know.
A junk on fire. A dog in the water. Blood on the snow.

In China seas . . .
Old movie posters, kimonas, ivory flesh, incense and feuding tongs,
In China seas . . .
Mandarins, porcelain, chop sticks, tea houses and quivering gongs.
Assassins still prowl, noose in yellow hand.
A single pebble on the yellow sand.

How the nubile geishas love the foreign dog.
The year of the flesh, the dawn of the fog.
The excruciating death of a thousand cuts,
And the night of the long knives when every peasant's door shuts.

In China Seas . . .
Shrimp nets transparent as the shrimp they catch . . .
In China Seas . . .
Thousand year eggs take a long time to hatch.
Judge Dee sleeps but the dragon wakes,
Fu Man Chu, you made one mistake . . .

The old man sits in the Chinese takeaway,
Wearing bedroom slippers and boiling peas.
As he makes up my order he gives me a smile
And says it really means, 'Fung's garage,'   in Cantonese.

HEARING VOICES AGAIN

'Greetings to the Tin Man,'
Said a voice from within.
'Speak up, could you,' I said,
'There's a terrible din.'

'Greetings to the Tin Man,'
Said a voice from without.
'OK, got you now,' I said,
'You don't have to shout.'

'Greetings to the Tin Man:
I'm the voice of the Nine.
So how're you feeling today?'
Said, 'Thanks, I'm feeling fine.'

'Muse, think and ponder,
And inwardly digest.'
'Scuse me for asking,' I asked,
'Is this some sort of test?'

'No, school is over, Tin Man.'
I said, 'Tell me something new.
I may be halfway simple
But I've read a book or two.'

'Then read your future, Tin Man.
Tell me what you see.'
'I see a crying giant
Who looks a lot like me.'

'Crying for what, Tin Man,
The halt, the blind and the lame?'
'All those, of course,' I said,
'Plus myself, plus my dog, plus a dame.

'Plus a dame made of fury and folly,
Plus a game with top-loaded dice.
But it's the only one in town,
So spare me your no-doubt well-meaning advice.'

'Farewell, then, oh Tin Man,'
Said the voice of the Nine.
'Get back to you later,
When we've got a better line.'

AND IN ANOTHER TOWN

On the Ramblas in Barcelona
Is a cafe where all the girls go.
I think it was called the 'Paradiso . . . '
Or something like that, something like that.
We all used to meet there after the fight,
Never such colors, never so bright.
I don't know why I remember it all
Or bother to write it all down,
For like the man said, it was a long time ago
And in another town.

On the Ramblas in Barcelona
Is a tavern that I used to know.
I think it was called 'San Francisco . . . '
Or something like that, something like that.
They finally fired that drunken waiter—
I heard he died in Badahos later.
There was often a girl to share the wine
How sweetly the young wine went down.
But like the man said, it was a long time ago
And in another town.

On the Ramblas in Barcelona
Is a hotel where we used to stay.
I think it was called the 'Meson Del Rey,'
Or something like that, something like that . . .
They watered the streets with patched-up hoses,
The gypsy from Jaen sold yesterday's roses.
Then you got married and Freddie got rich.
One by one we all settled down.
But like the man said, it was a long time ago
And in another town.

OLAFFSON'S

It's a quarter to one by my railroader's watch;
Got the old Sunday blues something cruel.
I'm lying on my bed in the Lonestar Motel
Wondering why I was born such a fool.

Last nite I stepped into my one-button roll
And dusted my Mexican hat.
Then I took myself over to Olaffson's Bar
Which is where all the action was at.

And the action I mean is the gambling kind,
And the name of the game was straight stud.
They weren't playing marbles so I stayed off the sauce,
Just a double to settle the blood.

At the end of an hour I'm a C-note ahead,
Which is just where I wanted to be.
See, I needed that hundred to get back my truck;
The Cale boys don't fix things for free.

I excuse myself nicely and head for the bar
Where I order the last of the night.
I'm dreaming of Monday and hitting the road
When a voice says, 'Hey, Cowboy, got a light?'

You can finish the rest of the story yourself,
And you won't have to go back to school.
She took every penny and I took first prize
In being the world's greatest fool.

TRAPPED IN THE BRUNSWICK TAVERN

Octoberfest on Bloor Street.
Stopped by the Clifford for a bite to eat.
The chef dropped something in the goose-grease
That had wool, but it sure weren't sheep.
A teenage junkie just outa Kingston Pen
Tried to peddle me some catnip cheap.

Octoberfest on Bloor Street!
Marched to the Brunswick where the elite don't meet.
Three fat Krauts in leather shorts
Played 'Eidelweiss' all night.
While I sat and drank Blue Label,
And considered my desperate plight.

Trapped in the Brunswick Tavern!
Trapped in a checked red shirt!
Trapped in a red ski parka—
I only laugh when I hurt.

Trapped in the Brunswick Tavern!
Trapped in Doctor Marten shoes!
Trapped in Canada now,
Trapped by the Bloor Street blues.

Octoberfest on Bloor Street!
Can't you see those hordes of dancing feet?
All the singing kiddies, the token Spade
Playin' the trumpet at the head of the parade.
Also, catnip ain't that bad a smoke
Once you get past that first, awful, poke.

LOVE IN THREE ACTS

Act I, Scene I — a party in Chelsea.
Terribly elegant, terribly gay.
Enter the hero in search of his hostess,
Enter the heroine, decides he will stay.

Act I, Scene 2 — just after the party.
Alone on a balcony facing the park.
Long-shot of traffic, sounds of rain falling,
Close-up of two cigarettes in the dark.

Act II, Scene I — A restaurant foyer.
Enter the husband, 'Well, quite a surprise.'
Terribly civilized, feelings well hidden,
Shadow of loneliness deep in his eyes.

Act II, Scene 2 — A bedroom in Chelsea.
Heroine worried she's done the wrong thing.
Hero consoles her, tells her he loves her,
Second act curtain sweeps down from the wings.

Act III, Scene I — a morning in Chelsea,
Terribly sunny, terribly gray.
Close-up of letter, scattered in fragments,
Close-up of tickets, torn once, thrown away.

What say the critics of this entertainment?
'Terribly comical? Terribly gay?'
'Tenderly written and movingly acted?'
'This sort of thing couldn't happen today?'

SHE WORE A BLACK BERET

The magic of first love,
So said a knowing friend,
Is in its ignorance
That it can ever end . . .

She wore a black beret
And smoked Du Maurier,
She was the fancy of my freshman year.
Her sandals were hand-made,
Her dangling earrings jade,
Her coolness as thin as a veneer.

She wore a black beret,
Got post-cards from Calais,
She was the fancy of my freshman year.
She scribbled in a pad
Her couplets sweet and sad
While sipping from a stein of German beer.

A touch of Kahlil Gibran
After class was out,
A hint of Chanel Number Five—
There was a lot of that about.

She wore a black beret,
It seems like yesterday,
She was the fancy of my freshman year.
Relentless years roll on,
The corner bar has gone,
And so has all the truth that seemed so clear.

But not to worry, dear,
There's one thing still is true:
I was, those years ago,
As obvious as you.

THE 'BAR OF THE MIDNIGHT SUN'

When I first shipped up to Nome, Alaska,
I was in the whole-selling trade.
There was a bunch of Eskimos, a few hundred whites,
A couple of Chinese and one Spade.

Now the Spade was called 'De Shadow,'
And he was the only law that Nome had got.
When he finally passed away from drinking too much,
Well you couldn't blame him a hell of a lot.

Now the oldest saloon in Nome, Alaska,
Was the 'Bar of the Midnight Sun.'
As soon as the whites went home for the night,
Then the locals came in for their fun.

The live entertainment nightly
Consisted of Bob and his purty wife Beth
Getting some half-breed stinking drunk,
Then kicking the poor Injun to death.

Now 'De Shadow,' who was the law, remember,
Got fatigued sweeping up the dead bucks.
So he tole Big Bob and his purty wife Beth
From then on to wear muckalucks.

After that the entertainment nightly
Was merely a harpoon fight or two.
And trying not to listen to the midget violinist
Who only played 'Sioux City Sue.'

. . . the old days, the dead days, the done days . . .
   Sure is thirsty work talking about the past . . .
   Why, thank you, Son, don't mind if I do,
   For a tenderfoot you're learning pretty fast.

THE PROPHET

See, I wanted to be a prophet,
A second Elijah but higher.
And come wandering out of the Sinai Desert
With my big brown eyes on fire.
A robe of rags and a bleeding heart,
Beggar's bowl and an alchemist's chart—
I'd be son of a king and I'd play the part . . .
For ever . . .

See I wanted to be a poet,
A delicate flower to handle.
I'd write about adolescent pain
By the light of a dying candle.
Barefoot girls in black berets,
Long lost Greenwich Village days,
We'd drink New York State beaujolais
For ever . . .

As water finds its level in its journey to the sea,
I too found my level, and it's not in Galilee.
It's in this noisy city trying to finish up on time
Another page of empty verse, another instant rhyme.

See I wanted to be a writer
And live in a left bank hovel.
Scott and Ernest down the hall,
They wept when they read my novel.
Drink all night at the Cafe Flore.
One last dance with the local whore,
Hail a cab and go to war . . .
For ever . . .

HALLOWEEN KISSES

Oh, oh, oh: what a mad scene.
Halloween, but not the Halloween
Of those ancient days of my youth,
When me and my little sister Ruth,
Wrapped in Mummy's best percale sheets,
Wandered the friendly neighborhood streets.

Trick or treat for an apple,
Or a handful of red jelly beans . . .
Black and orange were the kisses
Of those long-ago Halloweens . . .

Oh, oh oh: what a mad scene.
Grown-up treats this Toronto Halloween.
Me 'n ol' Daryl on the prowl,
Watchin' the locals tryin' to raise a howl.
Touch of class in an English-style pub,
Looking for ass in a rock 'n roll club.

Bought a policewoman a Bloody Mary;
Bought a skeleton a beer.
Danced a tango with a vamp
Till her apeman boyfriend appeared.

Struck out with a passing vampire,
Got nowheres with this cowgirl, too.
But I gotta 'yes' from a nurse in a dress
She musta stuck on with glue.

Me and the nurse played doctor,
Not only my temperature rose.
'n when she limped out in the morning,
I said, 'That's the way she goes.'

A different sort of kisses;
Did they taste as sweet?
I'll answer that foolish question
The next time that we meet.

DUTCH TREAT

On my second day in Dutchland I had me a date.
I was sitting at the bar where she told me to wait.
I know the whole thing sounds pretty banal,
But I was watching this boat sail up a canal.

And then she came running over the bridge
Like the Second Highlanders storming Vimy Ridge.
She looked a mite touched, if truth be told,
But I did some touching too before that night was old.

Oh oh oh my little Dutch treat,
Living and loving and laughter.
Right out of some crazy Hans Brinker spin-off
Where everyone was happy ever after.

The madness all started the night before
At the 'Exit' club, when I strolled in the door.
Some little geezer was getting in her hair,
She looked for some help and saw me standing there.

Now I'm not what you'd describe as petite,
In a dark alley I'm what you don't want to meet.
So the Sad Sack splits and the femme says, 'Sport,
You just got the job as this lady's escort.'

So if you ever go to Dutchland, you better beware
Of wild-eyed ladies with long blond hair.
Before you pack your skates you better think twice,
Their national sport they don't do on ice.

Oh oh oh my little Dutch treat,
Sweetly nutty as the day is long.
Did you ever find anyone, anywhere,
Who understood your song?

RAINED OUT IN RAPID CITY

I got off the bus where coach tole me to,
Opposite the park I had me a shake.
I still was the first in the locker room,
Those old habits is sure hard to break.

I was greasing my glove for the umpteenth time
And jawing with a lefty called Prof
When the man in blue comes in soaking wet
And says, 'Sorry, boys, gotta call it off.'

Rained out in Rapid City,
The umpire sed no play.
Rained out in Rapid City,
So there ain't gonna be no ball game today.

Now I'm readin' a comic in the motel room,
Wondering what in hell to do.
I could take a stroll to the Ree-alto,
But it don't open til two.
Anyways it's showing 'The Mummy's Curse,'
And I seen it a million times.
I might mosey down to Ed's poolhall
But the locals only shoot for dimes.

I could write a letter to my sweetheart
But I can never think of nothing to say.
There's that waitress down at the Bar-B-Cue,
But she tole me she's working today.

I could wash out a couple of tee shirts
And hang 'em on the line to drown,
Or just sit here lookin' out of the window
Watching all that moisture come down.

BOTTLE WISDOM

My ol' Sears separator finally folded up on me
When I was tryin' to get the hog mash mixed.
I tole the Missus there was nothin' more that I could do
Until I got that tin-assed nuisance fixed.

It looked like all she needed was a fan belt and a pin
And so I had a beer to pass the time
Till Fred got round to openin' up his hardware after lunch,
And swapping whoppers with a pal of mine.

So suddenly this out-of-date banana next to us
Addressed these queries to his umpteenth drink:
'Is there a rubber plughole in the ocean of desire,
Am I becos I am becos I think?

'How come one sort of woman just goes crazy over me,
And where does all the snows of April run,
And why do all my women always leave me in the end?
If cats have nine lives, why do dogs have one?

'How come I've hated Christmas ever since I was a kid,
And did they ever find that missing link?
If death comes after life then does life come after death?
Oh magic crystal, tell me what you think.'

His glass declined to answer and so I piped up instead:
'Say, stranger, take a rest from all that stuff.
Restrict yourself to fundamentals, like the Bible says,
Like, have you had too much or not enough?

'Don't clutter up your brain with tricky questions for some quiz.
Don't look for answers you don't need to know.
The only problem worth the posing I now put to you:
Should we have one more before we go?'

FAT CITY

I was on the road to Fat City
And I stopped off on the way.
I needed a break and a bite to eat
Cause I'd drove ten hours that day.

I left the heap at Clark's Garage
And tole 'em to check the spare.
Booked a room at the 'Bide-A-Nite'
And brushed what was left of my hair.

Sign across the road said, 'Silver Spur,'
'We serve cocktails 2 til 2.'
Cocktail I had was mostly H20—
Won't tell you what I found in my stew.

Then a local yokel took me good
Hustlin' on the pinball machine.
After buying drinks all nite for this gal
She took off with a bone-head Marine.

The bed I slept in had more lumps
Than the Army's cream of wheat,
And when I glimmed the padded bill,
Buddy, my joy was complete.

I paid the ransom for my car
Which left my wallet a mite depressed.
Sign beside the road outa town said,
'Friendliest Little Town In the West.'

I asked a 'bo who was hikin'
The name of that chiseling town.
When he says they call it Fat City
I figure I've picked up a clown.

But then I gets to thinking,
He ain't so stupid, that bum,
It might not have been fat for me
But it sure were fat for some.

KEEPING THE FAITH

I'm sitting and I'm sweating in a tin bar near the border,
Sharing a bottle of cold Carta Blanca with my memories.
Once in a while I buy a beer for the fat bartender,
And once in a while the fat bartender does the same for me.

I don't know what he's waiting for, it could be just manana,
Or a car with a drunken millionaire who's gonna stop one day.
He'll have a beautiful, bored blond gringa who's lookin' for a change
Of pace,
She'll say, 'Vamos, amigo,' then they'll all drive away.

But I don't need no crazy dream cause I know what I'm waiting on,
It's a two-hundred dollar check from my old pal Smokey McGee.
And that's gotta be about as safe as US money in the bank,
Cause we've been drinkin' buddies since we met in '63.

We was workin' in a run-down, one-pump garage out on Highway 104,
Just ten miles north-east of Tucson, and the very last I heard
He'd bought himself a truck or two and found himself a Cherokee girl—
I know he'll send the dinero the very day he gets the word.

See I was makin' a quiet little run from Tampa through Nogales,
I was supposed to meet a Mexican gent in a field near Monterrey.
I had this little package they'd requested me to deliver,
It wasn't strictly legal but hell tell me what is today.

But someone musta had a loose mouth or else couldn't hold their juice.
Or it coulda been some dirty little stoolie after a piece of the reward,
Because the Federalies flagged me down and tore up my old De Soto,
And two hours mas tarde they found it taped behind the running board . . .

Well I settled out of court cause that's the Mexicali way,
But after that I wasn't what you'd call a man of means.
But I had a little stash that I kept down inside one boot,
And that's kept me going for quite a while on beer and refried beans.

So all I gotta do now is hang on and keep the faith,
Cause I know my drinking buddy, my old amigo Smokey McGee,
I just know that lop-eared, bandy-legged son of a woman-chasing fool,
I know my viejo compadre is gonna keep the faith with me.

So I'm sitting and I'm sweating in a tin bar near the border,
Sharing a bottle of cold Carta Blanca with my memories.
Once in a while I buy a beer for the fat bartender,
And once in a while the fat bartender does the same for me.

THE 'OK BAR'

You know that stretch of highway linking Pueblo to Cheyenne,
I been working there since summer as a truck-stop handyman.
I showed on time, I got a raise, I bought myself a car,
And my sweetheart is a cocktail waitress down at the 'OK BAR.'

I was lunching today in the 'Aero' cafe when the Law steps in for a beer.
He didn't say nothing but his red old eyes held a message that was loud
and clear.
I could hear him think as he sipped his drink and it didn't take a
crystal ball to see.
That soon he'd send off a wire or two, then he'd come looking for me.

Well it's happened before and it'll happen again,
But that don't make it fun.
I've been tracked down in one more town
When the good times have just begun.
So I'll pack my bags and I'll hit the road
Making tracks to oblivion,
For it seems your past is gonna get you at last
No matter how hard you run.

Just one mistake, that's all it takes, and they make you pay and pay.
I'll have this quick one with you, friend, then I'll be on my way.
It's funny but what I'll miss the most is just sitting in my car
Waiting for my sweetheart to come off work down at the 'OK Bar.'

LAST PORT OF CALL

I'm taking the 'Molly' easy up the coast,
Headin' two points off the setting sun.
The lights of Rio are fading in the west,
Two old-timers on their last run.

She was built in Nantucket before the War—
That's the First World War I mean.
I signed on in Tampa as a cabin-boy
The day I turned sixteen . . .
The day I turned sixteen.
My poor old Ma didn't want me to go
But my Pa said, 'Ethelda, let the boy be.
I want none of mine on no assembly line,
Look what it done to me.'

So it's one last bottle down at the 'Seven Seas,'
And sure as hell one last brawl.
One last watch in a freshening breeze,
One last port of call . . .
One last port of call.

She's three thousand tons of old tin can
And her paintwork's a hell of a sight.
She rolls just a bit in a following sea
And she ain't exactly watertight.
But if Scotty in the hole keeps feedin' her coal
She'll go steaming on all night.

My eldest boy's got a farm in Maine
And he writes there's a room for me.
He says in the spring when the wind bends the trees
It looks like the sea.
But how'm I gonna tell my grandchild on my knee
What it was really like on the Panama run
Rolling in a following sea . . .
Rolling in a following sea.

LETTER TO THE BIG CITY

I've covered this lonesome planet
Hunting the rainbow scam.
Never did make too much bread,
Let alone my jam.

I followed the smell of money
Like a starving gigolo.
Now I'm gonna stay at home
'N watch the alfalfa grow.

    I'm not going back on the game, partner,
    So don't come looking for me, all right?
    I'm a changed man, I'm perfectly happy
    Shooting dollar pool on Saturday night.

    I'm not going back on the hustle, partner,
    I'm not budging from this rocking chair.
    Promise me fame or a beautiful dame,
    It ain't no use 'cause I won't be there.

I'm through with conning the patsies,
Done with hustling the scene.
I've grown grey before my time
Tracking that elusive green.

So I took a slow train to nowheres,
But partner, don't get me wrong,
I enclose my P.O. box number
In case a real sucker comes along.

LAUGHING DAUGHTER

She was born near the Great Water,
Her name was Laughing Daughter.
Her father was a chieftain of the Sioux.
Her mother was a princess of the mightly Mohawk Tribe,
So that made her a rightful princess too.

But many snows have melted since she left that Athabascan shore
She's seen a lot of sidewalks since, and they don't call her princess anymore.

Her father worked for Hudson's Bay
Until he showed up drunk one day,
After that he never worked again.
Her mother finally took her south to live in Battleford,
A treeless city in an empty plain.

But many moons have faded since she left that Athabascan shore.
She's known a lot more drunken men, and
                    they don't call her princess anymore.

The daughter of the noble Sioux
Has one good pair of high-heeled shoes.
She wears a necklace made of tortoise shell.
The chieften's blanket that she sits on as she combs her hair
Is torn, and stained with last night's Muscatel.

And many tents have folded since she left that Athabascan shore.
She's turned a lot of two-dollar tricks, and
                    they don't call her princess anymore.

And the loons don't cry on the lake anymore;
The geese never pass in the fall.
The wind doesn't sing through the spruce anymore;
The whipperwills no longer call.
The old men don't doze in the sun anymore;
The fires in their lodges are cold.
The children don't sit at their feet anymore;
The last of the tales has been told.
The wolf doesn't howl in the mist anymore;
The bear doesn't fish in the stream.
The hawk doesn't circle the hills anymore;
Except once in a while
In an Indian Princess' dream.

NITE MAN

I'm holding down the desk most evenings
In a rattrap that caters for strays.
It's just across from the station,
And we've both seen far better days.

The Frenchie on the first floor
Keeps having her family in for tea.
She's sure got a lot of cousins,
And one of them's a bloody Chinee.

There's a widow on the third floor
With a frantic case of the hots.
So I send up old Shakey the bellhop . . .
Hope he's had his tet'nus shots.

    It's fun being a nite man, a nite man, a nite man,
    Renting rooms in an uptown fleabag to faces without a name.
    It's fun being a nite man, a nite man, a nite man,
    The more folks come and go, the more things stay the same.

The Nancies on the fourth floor
Are playing me for a beginner.
OK, everyone cooks in their rooms,
But they're doing take out dinners.

The poker game in 202
Calls down for another bag of ice.
For disturbing my sensitive reflections,
I'm billing the bastards double price.

MA

Morning in Morinville . . .
Ice on the ground.
Not much of a morning,
Not much of a town.

Morning in Morinville,
Breakfast is glum.
The house on the prairie
Is missing its Mum.

Smudge of flour on her cheek,
Kitchen smelling of cinnamon and cloves,
Checkered cloth on the kitchen table,
Eggs over easy 'n' fresh-baked loaves.

But dog turds on the floor—
Ma wouldn't allow that.
Empties in the bathroom—
Ma wouldn't allow that.

Breakfast tea from dirty mugs,
Baloney fried in yesterday's fat,
Muddy workboots in the house—
Ma certainly wouldn't allow that . . .

But where is Ma?
Gone east.
When is Ma coming back?
When quiet sleeps the beast.

And where is Boy?
Headin' west.
And when is Boy coming back?
When the wind has blown the last
Bit of broken shell from the nest.

Morning in Morinville,
The pick-up won't start.
Frost on the windscreen,
Ice in my heart.

DAY TRAIN TO KINGSTON

An ordinary town, Kingston,
One good restaurant, a quiet port,
The hospital, the university,
A penitentiary and a fort.

An extra-ordinary girl on the day train to Kingston,
Long blond hair and huge brown eyes.
Half-woman, half-child, on the day train to Kingston,
So I sat down beside her and prepared my opening lies:

'Tell me your simple story, sweet vision,
To where are you going, and why?'
She sat for a moment in silence,
And watched telephone poles going by.

'I am going to visit my son,' she said.
'He's asleep and they can't wake him up.'
Then she smiled and poured out some coffee
And asked me if I'd like a cup.

'Is he waiting for some princess' kiss?' I enquired,
Doing my best to impress her with words.
'No, he over-dosed on some pills,' she replied,
'Now ain't that one for the birds?

'On his fifteenth birthday, we don't know what it was.
He's been in hospital for three months now.
If he does ever wake up, who will he be?'
And she brushed her hair back from her brow.

'Then my husband's agency was taken from him
Cause he spent all his time by his bed.
He blames himself and he's drinking a lot,
And that is my story,' she said.

'Now tell me your story, travelling man;
To where are you going, and why?'
I could find no answer to that simple question,
So I watched telephone poles going by.

I START TOMORROW
(Guru Song)

I got nothing to do for a month or two . . . I'm on vacation.
I got a big stack of good paperbacks to improve my education.
Thought I'd spend the days in helpful ways like self examination,
And then at night get my head right with some heavy meditation.

First thing today I went round the bay to a choice location,
Tuned my radio clock to the local rock and roll station.
It's nice and warm, so I'm giving the form some welcome solarization,
When along comes this eve whose bikini leaves nada to the imagination.

   I forgot my books, I forgot my plans,
   I start tomorrow being a better man.
   Today I got more important things to do,
   But I start tomorrow being a Guru.

My big mouth dried and I went cross-eyed clocking her perambulation,
She walked up to me 'n I couldn't help seein' her protruberations.
You'd never suppose she come from one of those under developed nations,
So anyway, I sez, muy buenas diez, how about some fraternization?

A poco of walk, a poco of talk, a mucho of celebration,
Esta noche al hotel they're having this swell flamingo demonstration.
She says, my names Barbee, I come from Darby, so skip the big oration,
Cause I'm only here for a week this year and I need resuscitation.

   I forgot my books, I forgot my plans,
   I start tomorrow being a better man.
   Today I got more important things to do,
   But I start tomorrow being a Guru.

OLD IRISH FOLKSONG

What's worse than being young, father?
You'll know when you start turning grey.
What's worse than turning grey, father?
Turning coward and running away.

What's worse than an empty plate, father?
An empty head, my pretty colleen.
What's worse than an empty head, father?
One full up with what might have been.

What's worse than an empty glass, father?
When the bottle is empty, too.
What's worse than an empty bottle, father?
When there's no one to share it with you.

What's worse than denying the needy, father?
Denying that faith will provide.
What's worse than denying your faith, father?
Denying you've ever denied.

What's worse than not having a lover, father?
Why, loving someone that's untrue.
What's worse than an untrue lover, father?
Being unfaithful to one who loves you.

And what's worse than being poor, father?
Being rich and not having a friend.
What's worse than not having a friend, father?
A song that won't come to an end.

SAVE THE HEARTS AND FLOWERS

Just another hour to kill in just another town,
But the same old longing for a glass of something cool.
I saw a lady through the window of a cocktail lounge,
So in I went 'n there beside her was an empty stool.

She had a face like an angel who'd fallen too far
And the eyes of a child who'd been running too fast.
Frozen on her cheek was one teen-age tear,
Crumpled on the bar was a letter from her past.

I thought, Careful, sailor, save the hearts and flowers,
    Cause she's heard it all before.
    Careful, sailor, save the hearts and flowers,
    She ain't falling for that one anymore.
    So listen, sailor, do yourself a favor,
    Pick up your feet and point 'em at the door.

She reminded me of someone that I'd never met,
A daughter I'd never had, a sweetheart I never knew.
I saw her chipped nail polish, I found my eyes were full,
I swear it wasn't the drink cause I'd only had a few.

For the first time in years I opened up my heart,
And out poured words long locked inside my head.
Suddenly I was blessed with the golden gift of tongues,
And when I fell silent the fallen angel said,

She said, Sorry, stranger, save the hearts and flowers,
    Cause I've heard it all before.
    Sorry, stranger, save the hearts and flowers,
    I ain't falling for that one anymore.
    So listen, stranger, do us both a favor,
    Wrap up your heart and walk it out the door.

THE BORING OLD FART'S LAMENT

OH OH OH I don't want to get old
And huddle in the corner in a cap.
Playing cribbage with another old fart
And listening to his boring old crap.

About the Wembley Cup Final in '32,
About his old age pension being late.
About the postcard he got from Walla Walla
From his son who's doing so great.

OH OH OH don't cry in your beer, Joe,
It's watery enough as it is.
OH OH OH don't say I told you so,
And wipe that smile off your phiz.

OH OH OH I don't want to get old,
With an old man's aches and pains.
Take an hour to get up the stairs,
Hurt everywhere just before it rains.

OH OH OH I don't want to get old
And eat lunch at an Old Folk's club.
And have to dance the hokey-cokey
With some varicosed-veined old tub.

    Debil is you listening, Debil, is you there?
    I'll make you a bona fide deal.
    You can take my soul down to your black hole,
    Leave me looking as young as I feel.

OH OH OH I don't want to get old
And go to Southend for the day.
Sitting on a bus singing sad old songs,
Trying to keep the tide at bay.

I hear they got homes for old actors,
And for veterans of foreign parts.
But I bet there ain't no fucking home
For plain old boring old farts.

EACH DREAM HAS THE GIRL

There are many versions of the dream.
Sometimes I build a cabin by a stream, on my own land.
I fell the logs and square the ends to fit with my own hands.
Then build a lean-to roof, cut in a window and a door,
She makes some patchwork curtains and a carpet for the floor,
Then hangs up on the wall a set of antlers that she's found,
And in the spring we plant some seeds in our little plot of ground . . .
There are many versions of the dream,
But each dream has the girl.

There are many versions of the dream.
Sometimes I find a sleepy town left over from the past,
And right away I get this feeling I've come home at last.
It's got a corner drugstore where I know I've been before,
I even know the town hall clock hasn't worked right since the war.
I get a job in the one garage and meet the boss's wife,
Then one day her big city sister drives into my life.
There are many versions of the dream,
But each dream has the girl.

There are many versions of the girl.
Sometimes she is the girl next door, the one who never was,
The kind of girl who never changes no matter what she does.
Sometimes she is the drifting kind and just a little soiled,
A waitress at a drive-in workin' hard at bein' hard-boiled.
Sometimes I hear her calling from the next bar up the line;
Sometimes she seems so close that I can almost call her mine.

There are as many versions of the girl
As there are unbuilt homes by mountain streams.
As there are men who sit in quiet corners,
Taking comfort from a glass of dreams.

CAPTAIN FUDGIE AND SERGEANT SPARKLE

It's a hot summer nite in downtown Sac
And the word goes out to grab a six-pack
And follow the gang down to 21st and C.
Cause the girls are playing ball up at City Park,
And they're gonna get started soon as it gets dark.
So if you want a laugh or two, string along with me.

It's just before the game, and what do I hear?
It's an ice cream wagon and it's drawing near;
It's Captain Fudgie and Sergeant Sparkle, making their evening call.
They're two fat ladies who got that way
By drinking up their profits every day;
Captain Fudgie and Sergeant Sparkle, coolest of them all.

The 'Aero Cafe' team is the one in white,
They're playing the girls from the 'Tavern' tonight;
Two tough sides fighting it out for the top.
According to the latest dope I heard
The 'Aero's' fielding foxy Gwen at third
And with Big Jude pitching, they're gonna be hard to stop.

And inbetween innings, what do I see?
An ice cream wagon, parked in front of me.
It's Captain Fudgie and Sergeant Sparkle, making their evening round.
They got drumsticks and Mello-Rolls,
Hot fudge sundays in cardboard bowls,
Captain Fudgie and Sergeant Sparkle, coolest gals in town.

Oh Captain Fudgie, my Captain Fudgie,
With your truck of goodies for sale
On a hot summer nite up at City Park
You're like Florence Nightingale.

Oh Sergeant Sparkle, my Sergeant Sparkle,
I know how much you like the beer.
It's easy to laugh sitting in the stands,
So pay no attention, hear?

Captain Fudgie and Sergeant Sparkle,
Accept this salute from a fan:
I award you this silver ice cream scoop
For outstanding service to man.

SECOND FLOOR FRONT

In a second floor room down on Ninth,
One flight up from the Greek bottle store,
Right across from a house where O. Henry once slept,
But O. Henry don't sleep there no more . . .

In a second floor room in the front,
Lay a waitress observing the rain.
She once loved a man, then the world went all wrong,
Now here she was, loving again.

    The light from the Greek's neon sign
    Bathed her in gold as she lay.
    Her lover cried out in his sleep,
    She kissed all his nightmares away.

    A tenderness born out of pain
    Shook her like wind bends the hay.
    The tenderness turned into sleep,
    The night slowly turned into day.

For a second floor front down on Ninth,
The awakening will come all too soon.
For come morning the Romeos sneak down the stairs,
And they wait for the next restless moon.

Yes it's morning when sports take their leave
Of young country girls brushing their hair,
And of sleepy-eyed dancers and hung over strays.
And of waitresses too quick to care.

THE BIRD BAR

Well I'm minding my business, as usual,
In a cantina called the 'Bird Bar.'
There's a wet-back asleep in one corner
With his arms round a broken guitar.
The bird that the bar was named after
Was a one-legged blackbird who drank.
I figured it must have a problem
So finally I asks it point-blank,

I says, why do you drink, Maria?
You know it ain't good for you.
Ain't you got no amigos to visit?
Can't you find nothing better to do?
If you go on like this, Maria,
Manana you'll wake up dead.
There was a pause for refreshments,
Then, sadly, she nodded her head.

It was later, much later, that evening,
When Maria gives out with a croon.
I was watching a saturated gringo
Eat a soft-boiled egg with no spoon.
I'd emptied a jug of 'Green Fish' gin
And the whole room was starting to sway.
That stuff had me thinking in Spanish
Cause I swear I heard that bird say:

She says, why do you drink, compadre?
You know it ain't good for you.
Ain't you got no amigas to visit?
Can't you find nothing better to do?
For what are you seeking, compadre?
Or have all your dreams gone dead?
Was it because of some woman?
And, sadly, I nodded my head.

Maria, my little paloma,
All that I'm hoping to find
Is a bottle of something to hide in
That won't turn me totally blind.

So light up another Perfecto
And let's share this bottle of beer:
We're safe, my sweet senorita,
She'll never find us in here.

BELIEVE IT OR NOT

Believe it or not, but inside of this mass of muscles
Is a dancer. Oh, what a mover.
In Monte Carlo the Ballet Rambert is all the rage.
I leap, I spin, I soar, I fly across the stage.
(A numb Nijinski limps to a corner to cry.)
He hangs up his favorite shoes from a broken nail.
Weeping, he stumbles across the slanted floor.
Weeping, he pauses at the open door . . .
He looks back once, and then again,
And then into the night and rain
Goes the crippled faun to die.

Believe it or not, but inside this out-of-date sports coat
Is a singer. Oh, what a crooner.
At La Scala the Great Caruso gets an aria wrong.
From the wings comes one pure phrase of angel's song.
(A disbelieving 'Rico is shaken to the core.)
He shouts at the conductor, his legs go weak, he swears.
He opens up the silver locket that he always wears.
Inside a faded picture of his mother smiles at him.
A faded lock of once-brown hair is curled around the rim.
As he presses his lips to it,
He whispers, 'Momma mia, I quit.
Pagliacci laughs no more.'

. . . that lonely lady standing by the stairs,
What dreams of beauty when she says her prayers?
That poet staring into inner space,
What private fame behind his public face?
And in the bliss of just enough to drink,
An unseen grip hits the baby pink.

Believe it or not, but behind this second-rate talent
Is a comic. Oh, what a jester.
It's backstage at the famous Radio City Music Hall.
As Benny puts his fiddle away, a tearlet starts to fall.
('To be or not to be, aye, there's the rub.')
There's no one in the world who doesn't love the Litlle Tramp,
But he's just seen the big one, that's why his cheeks are damp.
Mary tries to comfort him but it's no use, he's done.
And Benny tears his name off dressing room number one.
The scattered fragments fall like snow.
'Happy New Year,' he murmurs low.
'Rochester, the "Friars Club." '

IT'S A SHAKER

Want a shaker?
Want a real pick-me-down?
Want the tonic of age?
Want to see a woman
Not through a glass, darkly,
But in a rage,
Starkly?

Then, my son,
My bonny young one,
See her for the first time
With her brand-new man.
Try that one on for size.
Try that one if you can.
See how that one fits.
Better open a bottle first
And have a couple of good, solid hits,

'cause it's a shaker,
It's an earth-quaker,
A natural disaster, a veritable rout.
'cause it's a hummer,
An absolute bummer,
The kind of revelation that I can do without!

And, my son,
It's even less fun
When he turns out to be
Everything you're not—
Like young, like super-cool,
A Sal Mineo she's got.
How she loves his jokes . . .
Better roll a bomber fast
And have a couple of good, solid pokes,

'cause it's a shaker,
It's a dam - breaker,
It's a million laughs and a very nasty trip.
Son, is it a downer;
I'm heading out of town or
I know I'll flip what little lid I've left to flip!

'cause it's a blancher,
It's an avalancher,
Another Krakatoa with no Jon Hall in sight.
Son, it's a shocker,
A positive rocker . . .
I wonder what the San Andreas Fault is doin' tonight?

MAGPIE WOMAN

In a half-a-dozen cardboard boxes
I packed away half-a-dozen years of love.
So into 'Farmer John's Fresh Farm Eggs'
Went a broken vanity, a token glove.

A picture of us in Barcelona,
Some notes from her first Spanish class.
And, from the Witch's, down the Broadway,
A necklace of emerald green glass.

Old Valentine's cards, my first letter,
A porcelain hand for her rings.
A chipped enamel cigarette case—
The incredible power of everyday things.

   The notebook was the worst of all.
   On an otherwise blank page,
   After some Spanish homework,
   About a muchacho's Christmas Eve,
   On an otherwise blank page,
   In an early morning scrawl,
   'I might leave.'

I packed half-a-dozen years of laughs,
Up in the freezing loft they went
Along with all the books Steve left behind
And Kelly's clothes and Matt's army tent.

Go get 'em moths, they're all yours,
Blouses and trousers and charity shop suits.
Gather ye dust, skirts and boleros,
Stockings, bandanas, caps and old boots.

So many belts! So many dresses!
Presents from me, presents from Mother.
Cookbooks and diaries, old theatre tickets,
Funny T-shirts from her funnier brother.

   The notebook was the worst of all.
   On an otherwise blank page,
   After some Spanish homework
   About a muchacho's Christmas Eve,
   On an otherwise blank page,
   In an early morning scrawl,
   'I might leave.'

Well, let me tell you this, Farmer John,
Whatever foolishness the future brings
I'm never gonna marry another magpie woman,
It's hell packing away her things.

TAKE ME BACK

My best pal went to Paris right after the War
Without knowing quite what he was looking for.
I guess he found it, cause he never came back.
I was going too, had my bags all packed,
At the last moment my girlfriend rang, in tears,
With some inside information that confirmed all her fears.
So I did what was then considered to be the right thing,
And I never got to Paris that, or any other, spring . . .

I want to go back again
To a place I've never been.
I want to fall in love again
With a girl I've never seen.

I want to drink again
Wine my lips have never tasted.
I want to live again
A life I just might have wasted.

So take me back to Paris, France,
Give me wartime wine to drink.
Take me back to gay Paree
When I was too young to think.

Bring me back that merry band,
Lean us 'gainst that marble bar,
Let her tuck her arm in mine
When the garcon says, 'Bon soir.'

Let us walk the Paris streets,
Kiss beneath the chestnut trees . . .
Silly for a man my age
To have to make up memories . . .
The strange thing is, when my old pal writes,
He wants to know about things back here.
About the old gang (just a few of us left)
About his old girl (she got married last year)
And how was I doing? Well, I'm doing OK;
With two lovely kids and a third on the way,
And if sales keep up til the new models are out,
We could swing that camper we been talking about.

So who's got the most to remember?
Who's having the happiest life?
Him in a cafe in Montparnasse,
Me on the porch with my wife?

I'm mostly content with my lot, I swear,
Most days I'm happy as a king.
But if only, if only, I'd been over there
Just for a few days that long-ago spring.

THE GIRLS WHO GO DIGGING FOR GOLD

Many tales have been told of the brave and the bold
Who deserted the big city's blare.
Who went chasing a dream to the Malamute stream
And the nuggets of paradise there.

Many yarns have been spun of huge fortunes hard-won
Neath the midnight sun's terrible cold.
But for true tales of greed, sing a different breed:
Sing the girls who go digging for gold.

For the girls who go digging for gold, for gold,
Never risk their pretty faces
Panning ore in Godless places,
Rubbing snow in frozen cheeks and sleeping in their clothes.
No, the girls who go digging for gold, for gold
Scan their brows for ageing traces,
Practicing their airs and graces,
Rubbing perfume on their wrists and powdering their nose.

So sing the girls who dig for gold, the gold that men have won.
In one mad, frantic, drunken night six months of gold dust gone.
Six months of bitter toil to rent an hour of tired charms,
Six months of blood to barter for an hour in perfumed arms.

The mountain men are gone now, gone the Cheechako,
Gone the tenderfoot and sourdough.
Gone the wild bonanza of the spring of '84,
Gone where all the Indian summers go.

But they will always be around, the girls who dig for gold,
Until the day the Great Creator finally breaks the mold.
Yes they will always be around as long as there are men
Who have to rent the tired face of passion now and then.

And the girls who go digging for gold today
Still put on their party dresses,
Still wear ribbons in their tresses,
Coax 'Perfesser' at the upright for their favorite tunes.
Have for sale the same caresses,
Tolerate the same excesses
As their sisters used to do in bare frontier saloons.

For the needs of a man, from Chinook or Japan
Are, exactly the same, give or take.
A new challenge to dare and a woman to care . . .
All the rest is just icing the cake.

What the hell do you do if you're one of that crew
With no woman in some windy town?
When the Blue Devils blow I know right where I go—
To the nearest gold-digger around.
Call 'em cold, call 'em hard, but they'll welcome you, pard,
Be you Momma's boy, misfit or clown.

MARIE ANTIONETTE

Marie Antionette Teresa Agatha Smith
Would you please believe
Manicurist and masseuse
And also tensions relieved

Had black eyes and dynamite dope
Tucked inside her high-heeled boot.
Won't say I got off on it
But I came down by parachute.

So we watched the Provincial Police
As they ultra-casually cruised by
Edmonton's famous international airport—
Could this face tell a lie?

    Fly to some wild blue yonder, babe,
    Babe, flee from your past,
    Faster than light or else it just might
    Catch up with you at last.

Your boyfriend scratched your car
Which is why you are where you are.
Scratched it with a hatchet, too,
And the following soiree came looking for you.

Brothers are handy things to have
When the time's come to cut and run;
Try the one busted for horse
(And busted by it, dear one.)

Just enough left of his head
To wheel four balding tires
Down country roads with a load
Of fence posts and baling wire.

Just enough left of his heart
To take in one young, bruised stray.
And not ask too many questions—
Hell the answers are clear anyway.

I must drop a card to the girls
Back at that shitty agency.
And get off a note to Sheila
Reminding her she promised to see
The garaging's paid on the Mustang.
(Bucket seats and gold hard top)
I'll drop a note to guess who, too.
Find yourself another sucker, Pop . . .

Wonder what I'll do tonight . . .
Wondering where it's happening in this town.
Must be a couple of swingers somewhere,
Someplace there's action going down.

Marie Antionette Teresa Agatha Smith,
Change your jungle but not your spots.
OK, OK, but what's a girl to do
With a permanent case of the hots?

SAYONARA, OKINAWA

If I ever go to Okinawa
To the town of Ishikawa
Anyone will tell you how to find the 'Bar Ritz.'
The coolie with no teeth
Serving saki half-asleep
Answers to the un-Chinese name of Fritz.
Anyway, if you do go there,
Have a San Miguel for me,
For I'm never gonna make it back,
Back to the East China Sea.
It's too late for going back,
You can't change history.

It was the end of World War II,
My discharge was coming through
But I had to go to hell and gone to get the bloody thing.
Five thousand miles away
To San Francisco Bay
From where I planned to give my girlfriend and my folks a ring.
See I wasn't going home
To my uncle's hardware store
And I had to tell my girlfriend Betty
I didn't love her any more.
Then I was going to turn around
And take the first ship back,
Back across five thousand miles
Of Pacific on the starboard tack.
Back to a little bamboo town
A promise to redeem;
Back to my Chinese sweetheart,
Back to my ivory dream.

Got discharged and then got drunk;
Got beat up by a big Bohunk,
Got rolled in San Francisco by a girl with silver hair.
Hungover, sick and broke
I hitched north to my folks,
Planning to work a month or two until I'd saved the fare.
It was a lot of money.
Everyone treated me swell.
My Ma couldn't stop spoiling me
Or my old Uncle Joe as well.
After a while I didn't think about her as much.
After a while I couldn't write her anymore.
After a while me and Betty got married.
After a while my uncle died and I took over the store.

Sometimes when my wife is going on at me
About something real important like the cost of freeze dried coffee
Or the latest cute thing that Ellen's baby said,
I sorta drift off in my head.
'You're not listening to me,' my wife says.
'Whenever you get that look on your face I know you're not listening.
Where do you go when you drift off like that?'
I say, 'Nowhere special, honey. Just day-dreaming.
Come on, I'll buy you a fancy cocktail across the street at the "Silver Spur".'

ROSIE, BLUE RIVER, THE JEWEL OF THE YELLOWHEAD
(With My Pard Rick)

I had to get over to the West Coast
To look up Larry Kyle.
He owed me sixteen hundred bucks
Which made it worth my while.
I had this cash-flow problem,
Decided to take a bus.
Boarded the Greyhound in Edmonton,
Indians and dust.

Rode that thing through the sleet and snow,
Alberta highway 5.
By the time we hit Blue River
I was glad to still be alive.
'Husky Truck Stop' — three a.m.
Should'a seen the state of the place.
A voice says, 'Nice hot coffee, sir?'
And my eyes light on her face . . .

She was pure homegrown mountain lady.
Hair down to her shoulders burning red.
Sparkle in her eyes to set you dancing.
Rosie, Blue River, Jewel of the Yellowhead.

I was on my third cup of coffee
When the bus pulled out of town.
I waved goodbye to Larry Kyle
And I was sixteen hundred down.
See I knew that Larry was shipping out
And that he'd be a year at sea,
But by then I knew that Rosie's man
Was inside doing three.

I found out Rosie had a child;
Found she was lonely, too.
So I hung around and dug myself in
Til summer was almost through.
I loved Rosie and she loved me;
Her half-breed boy called me Chief.
But John Running Fox got out in the fall
And there was gold on the first maple leaf.

John Running Fox was in for GBH;
He'd been in twice before.
No matter how much I loved Rosie
I loved living even more.

So when the autumn finally came,
At three a.m. one night
I caught the bus and didn't look back
Til Blue River was out of sight.

I'm gonna miss her black-haired boy,
Gonna miss her sweet caress.
Gonna miss her red hair on the pillow
The rest of my life, I guess.

Rosie, Blue River, the Jewel of the Yellowhead.

ROMEO

Once in a while
With no trace of a smile
She'd call me 'Romeo' — I
Dunno why.

Some (ex-) close friends of mine,
Seeking the ultimate line,
The final topper, the acme of gags,
The peak of hilarity, richest of rags,
Have had the brazen nerve to protest
She said it in some sort of cynical jest!

I pity those world-weary zombies,
As I deeply pity the Infidel Riff,
Eating his sheeps-eyes and yesterday's cous-cous:
Feed him Beluga, he wouldn't know the dif.
I pity, too , the deluded Rosicrucian,
Locked in some freakish idea of what's true.
Incapable of all simple belief
In the goodness of women and their inner virtue.

Now I admit, I admit
I'm lacking a bit
Of what the Spanish call savoir-faire.
I'm OK on the 'what,' I
Can manage the 'why,'
But I've always been weak on the 'where.'

Yes, I confess, I confess,
I'm sort of a mess
When it comes to erroneous zones.
I can't find all those parts
That I've seen on the charts
That elicit those rapturous moans.

So there is an outside chance
Those cocktail cynics could be right.
What I could do is ask her but
She ran away the other night.

That's the bad news, that's the shits.
That's the awful news, the pits.
That kind of news makes World War II
A footnote in the 'Bad News Review.'

The good news is, comparatively,
The loser she's with is older than me.
So at least she's not screwing some drop-out surfer
While his cheap patchouli incense smokes
And Mr. Hip pops an Ammie one-handed
And gives her another of his mind-blowing pokes.

Wherefore art thou esta noche, babe?
Dost still smell as sweet
Slouching down some suburban street?
Wherefore art thou,
Thou who call't me Romeo
Not so very long ago?
I dunno, I dunno, I dunno, and yet
I dost know you were no ball of fire yourself
But I never called you 'Juliet.'

EIGHT BEDS IN THE ROOM

There's this mission-run hotel
The locals call 'The Last Chance.'
It's in Scranton down on Center street
And it costs a quarter, in advance.

There is eight beds in the room,
The walls had once been green.
So's you couldn't steal the bulbs,
Over the beds was a chicken-wire screen.

Sign nailed to the wall said
'See the attendent for soap.'
To which some wit had added,
'Now that's what I calls hope.'

'No eating, drinking, spitting or swearing,
And at eight a.m. you leave.'
The same forgotten wit had added,
'From time to time, could I breathe?'

On the end bed sat Old Charlie,
Not eating, cause he had nothing.
Not drinking, cause he had even less.
Not spitting, cause he was dry as a miser's love,
But swearing a lot, due to all of the above.

On the second bed along lay Frenchy,
Lost in a tequila trance.
He was looking for his life story
In an old copy of 'True Romance.'

The third bed alone was still empty.
It was known as a bad luck bed.
A crazy Injun in it one night
Had tried to scalp his own head.

On the fourth bed a sailor snored.
Night before he'd staggered in mad.
A lady of the night up in El Dorado
Had took him for every nickle he had.
When he woke his joy would be complete,
Frenchy had just stole the boots off his feet.

On the fifth bed along,
Trying not to gag,
Big Swede was sneaking sips
Of 'Old Tawny' from a brown paper bag.
Shoot, that stuff was so darn sweet
You could smell it a mile away,
Even over the joint's normal aroma,
'Parfume de Y.M.C.A.'

Billy Boy was standing on the next bed
So's to be nearer the twenty-watt light.
He was sewing a hole in some underwear
The color of wet anthracite.

On the seventh bed along
A guy in a torn negligee
Was seriously tellin' the floor,
'Listen, I weren't always this way.'

On the eighth bed along a rube was tellin' the Momma's Boy on
the seventh bed that, one, he sure wished he'd shut up for a
change, two, he probably were always that way, and three, if
he could see his way clear to advancing him the small sum of
twenty cents American, he would repay him with a nickle inter-
est as soon as the First National Bank, of which the president
was a close personal acquaintance of his, opened for business
the following a.m.

There was eight beds in the room.

WHATEVER HAPPENED TO LARS?

I was doing a buddy a favor this time
(With a small something in it for me)
See he had a not crate to get out of the state
Which was exactly my cup of tea.

Without thinking I detoured down old 402—
What the hell, he was covering the gas—
I was seeking these friends right where Terre Haute ends,
All I found was some dead sassafras.

The feedstore was gone where their turn-off begun,
No more rusty old plows out behind.
I went blue in the face trying to track down a trace,
I thought I'd gone soft in the mind.

To one side of a diner two Gramps and a dog
Had a horseshoe pitch set in the dust.
So I parked in the shade 'n cooled off as they played,
Then said, 'Ain't interfering, I trust?

'But does either of you know what happened to Lars?
Guess it would be just after the War.
He was working at that there machinery repair,
His old woman helped out at the store.

'A big Swede with a beard, I was put in his care
For a year while I done my parole.
God-damn son-of-a-gun, I tried bribing the one
Honest cop in the Highway Patrol.

'Hell, I wasn't that bad but I wasn't that good;
But they swallowed me into the fold.
I repaid them all right by absconding one night
With a few items easily sold.

'So don't neither of you know what happened to Lars?
I was figuring to just say hello.
But their whole God-damned spread, the store and the shed,
Well they just couldn't get up and go.'

The most juvenile of the two ancients took aim,
Then he swatted a bug on his seat.
Then he tossed on a ring with a casual swing,
Then he spat in the dust at his feet.

'It's the old road you're wanting, if I read you right,
It's the one that runs up past the mill.
And she then takes a wind to the valley behind,
Sort of stepping her way down the hill.'

'Tell me, how do I get to the old road, then, Pop?'
The old cronies guffawed fit to bust.
While they sputtered and sneezed and they coughed and they wheezed,
The old hound rolled about in the dust.

Then one managed to gasp, his paroxysm run down,
'There is only one way that I know.
If you travel in time then you'll make out just fine,
Set your dial back ten years, and then go.

'Cause a new road has come and the old road has gone,
As has likewise that farm and that store.
As has likewise my home and Lake Winnacomb,
There ain't none of them there anymore.

'See they laid down this elegant eight-laned affair
With their bulldozers, concrete and stone.
Where that store of yours stood is a chalet of wood
Which sells soft frozen yoghurt in cones.'

Don't spend too much time on those old dusty roads
Or meandering down memory lane,
Don't wear out your boots on those old rural routes
For, like this high-class fellow said
In some library book I never read,
It's the shits trying to go home again.

THE 'PARADISE ROOM,' MONTMARTRE

Now there ain't many bars that deserve any stars
And that, sir, is something to grieve.
Casablanca had 'Rick's,' where time played its tricks,
But that was just make-believe.

But there was one saloon that really called the tune,
Run by me 'n Buster, an old pal of mine.
To wax eloquent, it was *the* spot for a gent
To sample the fruit of the vine.

We met in Paree musta been '53,
When the fuss in Korea was done.
Ol' Buster was still on the GI bill
And me — I was just havin' fun.

The bar's nom de plume was the 'Paradise Room,'
And it sported a western decor.
As I recall, saddles hung on the wall
And a wagon wheel over the door.

   You're right if you think that I'm partial to drink
   For I surely do love the juice.
   Some drink to remember and some to forget—
   We all have a different excuse.
   Do I drink to remember that 'Paradise' lost,
   Am I trapped in the dreams of the past?
   Do I drink to forget the one woman I loved?
   Well, anyway, this next one's my last.

See this number one Jane come in out of the rain
And Buster and I made our play.
When she settled for him I felt pretty grim
But what's a best friend gonna say?

And so the years passed full of drinking and laughs,
Full of music and talking and friends . . .
Then I neglected to pay the right gendarme one day
And the 'Paradise' came to an end.

Now there ain't any way to stop time's decay
And there's mornings I feel a mite frail.
But today I don't care cause I'm walkin' on air,
See I got this surprise in the mail.

A picture postcard and there was my pard
In front of a new 'Paradise.'
It's opening was planned and he needed a hand—
Well stranger I didn't think twice.

It's near Carson City which can be mighty pretty
With the Sierras just off to the west . . .
They sent me the fare and some greenbacks to spare.
They heard I was hurting, I guess.

   Yeah you're right if you think
   That I'm partial to drink,
   For I surely do love the juice.
   Some drink to remember and some to forget—
   We all have a different excuse.
   Do I drink to remember that 'Paradise' lost,
   Am I trapped in the dreams of the past?
   Do I drink to forget the one woman I loved?
   Well anyway this next one's my last.

THE CODE OF THE ROAD
(Apologies to Nelson A.)

'Never eat at a joint called Mom's,
Never play cards with a guy named Doc.'
If a widder-woman invites you home,
Prepare yourself for a hell of a shock.

Never go to bed with a whore called Sis,
Never shoot craps with a guy called Prof.
If you drop the soap at the YMCA,
Don't bend down if you got your trunks off.

Never hitch a ride through Alabam
Without a fiver in your kick.
Don't drink Old Spice aftershave,
Holy Christ, it makes you sick.

Keep outa Jefferson after dark.
In fact, avoid it in brightest day.
In fact, the best thing to do with Jefferson Mo
Is point your feets the other way.

Never get a shave at a barber school,
There's better ways of bleeding to death.
If you ever go through Evan's Pass,
Cross your fingers and hold your breath.

Never try panhandling in the rain,
Stay out of Kalamazoo.
Never get mixed up with a girl
Who's more mixed up than you.

Never take a tip from a racing tout
Says he's got a friend at the track.
Never lend a fiver till the end of the week,
You can get mighty grey waitin for it back.

Never go dancing in a blue suit
With a gal in an angora sweater.
If your guts is giving you trouble,
Lay off raw spuds and you'll feel better.

Never pick a fight with a one-armed man.
Whatever happens, buddy, you lose.
If they let you into the Teamster's Union,
Shut your mouth and pay your dues.

Never buy a drink for an Indian gent
Less you're partial to losing your hair.
The only time to draw to an inside straight
Is the day ten-spots fall from the air.

Never hop a freight when the signal's red.
Stay outa grape country in the fall.
Never hop a ride on a cattle train.
If you ain't snow-white avoid St. Paul.

But the best advice I got for you, friend,
Is never hit the road at all.
And if you got half a brain in your head
You'll never hit the road at all.

BALLADS OF A BENCH WARMER